Books by Stilton Jarlsberg, M.D.

THE ONE MINUTE MANGLER (with Kenneth Bleucheese, Ph.D.)

*Quickly Published Sequels
to the Best-Selling "One Minute Mangler"*

THE ONE MINUTE MANACLE: The Business of Bondage
THE ONE MINUTE MANATEE: Success for Seacows
THE ONE MINUTE MANDARIN: Ruling China in 60 Seconds
THE ONE MINUTE MANDIBLE: Sinking Your Teeth in Success
THE ONE MINUTE MANDOLIN: Success for the Plucky
THE ONE MINUTE MANDRILL: A Manual for Monkey Business
THE ONE MINUTE MANGER: An Efficient Christmas Story
THE ONE MINUTE MANGO: Enjoying the Fruits of Success
THE ONE MINUTE MANIC-DEPRESSIVE: Careers in Postal Service
THE ONE MINUTE MANICOTTI: Get Your Career Cooking
THE ONE MINUTE MANICURE: Success at Your Fingertips
THE ONE MINUTE MANIFOLD: A Career Tune-Up and Oil Change
THE ONE MINUTE MANITOBA: A Canadian Career Guide, Eh?
THE ONE MINUTE MANNEQUIN: Management Tools for REAL Dummies
THE ONE MINUTE MANNERISM: Twitch Your Way to the Top
THE ONE MINUTE MANSERVANT: Damnit, Leroy, Where's My Brandy?
THE ONE MINUTE MANTA RAY: Swim with the Sharks and Win
THE ONE MINUTE MANTIS: Don't Get Bugged, Get Even
THE ONE MINUTE MANURE: Putting the BS in "Business"
THE ONE MINUTE MENAGE-A-TROIS: Easy as One, Two, Three

Who Cut the Cheese?

**An A-Mazing Parody About Change
and How We Can Get Our Hands on Yours**

Stilton Jarlsberg, M.D.

This is a work of fiction. All characters, corporations, institutions and organizations are either the product of the author's imagination or, if real, are used fictitiously without any intent to describe their actual conduct.

Graphic images licensed from www.Clipart.com

For More Information About
Who Cut The Cheese?
visit www.CutCheese.com
or contact Stilton@CutCheese.com

Check out Stilton Jarlsberg's inspirational webcomic
at www.JohnnyOptimism.com

*Dedicated to all the working people
who feel like rats trapped in a maze,
yet never seek professional help
for this obvious psychosis.*

*"You mightn't happen to have
a piece of cheese about you, now?
No?
Well, many's the long night
I've dreamed of cheese
-- toasted, mostly --
and woke up again,
and here I were."*

—Robert Louis Stevenson, Treasure Island

----

*The cheese stands alone,
The cheese stands alone,
Hi-ho the derry-oh,
The cheese stands alone.*

- The Farmer in the Dell

Who Cut The Cheese?

CONTENTS

OUR BRAINS COME APART

The Simple-Minded and The Complicated

The four characters found in this story – the rats: Snitch and Scamper, and the teeny people: Hi and Ho – represent the *simple-minded* and *complicated* parts of our brains, regardless of our age, gender, race, or unmedicated mental condition.

Sometimes we behave like
Snitch
Who gets information about change
by fair means or foul, or
Scamper
Who scampers at full speed into action
and the occasional wall, or
Hi
Whose hysteria grows increasingly
shrill as he confronts change, or
Ho
Who learns that the best way
to find Cheese is to act like a rat.

No matter which part of our brains we use, there are two things *we all have in common:* our need to travel successfully through the maze of life...and the fact that 90% of our brains are water.

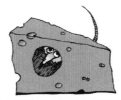

Behind The Story of The Story
Foreword by Kenneth Bleucheese, Ph.D.

I'm tickled pink to be taking you "behind the story of the story" of *Who Cut The Cheese?* because it means that another copy of this book has been sold, and my pile of Cheese has just gotten bigger. Of course, *your* pile of Cheese has just gotten smaller by exactly the same amount, meaning you need this book.

Or perhaps you received this book as a gift from a friend who is trying to give you a hint only slightly more subtle than taping a "loser" sign on your back. If this is the case, you *desperately* need this book. And probably less cowardly friends.

In either event, I've wanted to share this fabulous "Cheese" story ever since it first dawned on me that a tiny book with oversized print, wide margins, and lots of pictures would only take about a day to write.

Who Cut The Cheese? is a parable (Latin for *"terrible parody"*) in which four characters must find a way through a maze in their hunt for "Cheese."

But please keep in mind that this Cheese is actually *symbolic of the things that we all want out of life:* success and self-confidence, a nice house, a loving marital relationship, perfect children, a loyal dog, indoor plumbing, good Chinese food, several million tax-free dollars, and passionate red-hot sex with multiple partners.

The metaphorical Cheese could be your job, your relationship, your Horrible Secret— *anything* that makes you happy, no matter how unrealistic or sick. Pursuing this Cheese gives our lives meaning.

But finding your Cheese and then having it unexpectedly cut off can be absolutely devastating. Especially if it involved genitalia.

By the way, if you thought this book would actually help you find *real* cheese, well...*it's over in your supermarket's dairy section.* You can close up this book now and go back to watching the Cartoon Network. Glad to have helped.

The "Maze" in this story is symbolic of all the twisting, turning, confusing, mugger-filled blind alleys of Your Life.

A maze filled with incomprehensible dangers, sudden gut-wrenching turns, and walls which seem to be pressing in on you—tighter, *tighter*—squeezing the very air out of your lungs. Whew!

Most importantly, since you're being compared to a scurrying rat in this book, the whole "maze" analogy works like a charm.

As a well-paid professional counselor in Failure Management Skills, I've recited this Cheese story hundreds of times to groups all over the world. The response is always gratifying—especially in those countries that speak English.

Though it's almost impossible to believe, this simple Cheese story is responsible for getting people better jobs, helping them lose weight, and growing thick lustrous hair on bald heads.

What's more, this Cheese story has been credited with healing lepers, carrying children out of burning orphanages, and saving the Earth from a disastrous comet strike. If it were only a few pages longer, it might well raise the dead.

The book is divided into three sections. The first section, *A Reunion,* takes place in a hotel bar. It introduces you to a group of friends who share their feelings about the changes occurring in their lives and careers.

The next section is *The Story of Who Cut The Cheese?* which wasn't long enough to turn into a book on its own without considerable padding. In *The Story* you'll meet two rats and two teeny people who are faced with change. Not to give away the ending or anything, but the two rats do beautifully while the teeny people suffer the torments of the damned because they fall back on old behaviors instead of buying self-help books.

The third section of the book, *Another Round, Bartender,* returns us to the hotel bar where the friends have soaked up so much alcohol that the Cheese story is actually starting to sound good to them.

Some people may want to stop reading this book immediately after *The Story of Who Cut the Cheese* so that they may consider what it means to them personally. Or perhaps they just have short attention spans.

Others will want to immediately read *Another Round, Bartender* to share the insights that the friends have picked up from the Cheese story.

These insights will have even more appeal and meaning if you, too, are drinking large quantities of something flammable.

I hope that you'll re-read *Who Cut the Cheese?* over and over, and pick up something new each time. I hope you'll learn how to cope with change, and discover how to find the Cheese that will make your life joyous and fulfilling.

Failing that, feel free to take crayons and color in all the pictures. It's fun, it's therapeutic, and it will make it impossible for you to return this book for a refund.

Kenneth Bleucheese
San Quentin, California

Who Cut The Cheese?

A Reunion
Schenectady, NY

On a bleak Sunday, with dirty snow falling from a suffocating blanket of gray clouds, four friends gathered in the bar of the hotel where they were staying. They had not seen each other since high school, more than a dozen years ago, and the reunion would've been extremely happy if not for the actual circumstances.

"Jesus," said Norman, "I've been to some pretty ugly funerals in my day, but that one takes the cake! Poor Fred."

"Who talked the family into having an open casket service?" wondered Michelle. "A putty salesman?"

"It was probably the same guy who convinced Fred that he could repair his own riding mower without shutting off the engine," chuckled Biff.

"I'll never be able to watch the end of *Fargo* again," shuddered Naomi. "Hey Bartender! We need some drinks over here!"

A period of respectful silence settled over the group as the drinks arrived, as each pondered their own mortality and the wisdom of hiring a lawn service. But after a second round of drinks, and then a third, moods began to lift.

"Actually, this is probably the best career move Fred ever made," observed Biff. "He'd been fired by his firm, hadn't worked in a year, and didn't have a dime in the bank. Now his kids and widow will at least get a nice insurance check."

"I'll bet they get more than a fruit basket from the mower company, too," added Michelle. "Did you see the personal injury lawyer taking video of Fred's kids crying? That should bring in more money than *Avatar* did."

This brought a nice round of chuckles from the group, and another round of drinks from the waitress.

"Life sure doesn't turn out the way you expected," said Norman. "I'm 39 years old, still an assistant manager at BaggaBurger, and my only social life is visiting The Hair Club for Men."

"And who would've thought that I'd have gone through three divorces by now?" added Naomi. "My husbands knew I liked to sleep around when they met me – *then* they expected me to change!"

"Maybe that's been the problem for all of us," said Michelle. "We haven't achieved all we could in life because we've been afraid of change."

"That used to be my problem, too," said Biff. "But not anymore. In fact, my life is going so spectacularly well that even Fred's agonizing death can't keep the smile off my face!"

"But...Fred was your *brother!*" stammered a shocked Naomi.

"I told you I was doing great!" laughed Biff. "I'm rolling in dough, I live in a mansion, and I'm getting all the women I want!"

"What about your wife?" asked Norman.

"As far as I know, she gets all the women she wants, too," Biff winked. "You see, I've learned to see change in a whole new way – not as something to be

15

feared, but as something to be embraced! And I owe it all to one little story."

"What story?" Michelle asked.

"It's the story of *Who Cut the Cheese,*" Biff beamed, "and it's available now in better book stores and on eReaders nationwide!"

"Who Cut the Cheese?," laughed Naomi, "Just from the title, it sounds like an excellent value and a terrific gift idea!"

"You couldn't be more right," agreed Biff. "When I was first told the story of *Who Cut the Cheese*, I thought it was the dumbest thing I'd ever heard. I mean, next to sticking your head into a lawnmower. But when I thought about it, I realized that the simple lessons of the story could change my entire life. And they have!"

"Wow!" marveled Norman as he mouthed the words "another round" to the busy waitress. Then, "Would you tell us the shtory...uh, story?"

The others eagerly encouraged Biff.

"I'd be happy to," smiled Biff, sliding his hand across Naomi's supple thigh. "It doesn't take long to tell. It's just about the length of an extremely thin book!"

And as the drinks arrived, Biff began to tell his tale.

The Story of
"Who Cut The Cheese?"

Once upon a time, there were four little creatures who lived together in a giant maze. These little creatures spent their days searching the maze for pieces of cheese which would fill their bellies and give them pleasure and security.

Two of the creatures were rats named "Snitch" and "Scamper" and two were teeny people – human creatures who looked and behaved exactly like we do, with the exception of eating nothing but cheese and occasionally trying to "get lucky" with a rat. Their names were "Hi" and "Ho."

Because all four creatures were so small, it would be easy to ignore the things they were doing, and just leave some D-con out in hopes it would keep them out of the pantry. But if we look closer, especially with our reading glasses on, we'll be surprised at all of the things they have to teach us!

Each morning, the rats and the teeny people would wake up, stretch, find a wall to whiz on, then begin their daylong hunt for cheese.

The rats, Snitch and Scamper, having brains which looked and functioned much like the raisinets which frequently popped out of their other ends, had to rely on their instincts to find cheese. This involved a great deal of effort, a lot of trial-and-error, and a fair bit of dumb luck.

The teeny people, Hi and Ho, used their more complicated brains and sophisticated reasoning power to search for cheese. And for them, the cheese was *more* than cheese. It was Cheese with a capital "C" – and the Cheese represented not just food, but also a life of prosperity and happiness, much the way it does in Wisconsin.

The maze itself was a vast collection of twisting, turning halls and passageways, seemingly with no real beginning or end. In some parts of the maze, yummy bits of cheese could be found, left by the mysterious, unseen Cheesegiver.

In other parts of the maze, there were dark alleys, hidden trapdoors, and things that looked suspiciously like minotaur droppings. All in all, the maze was a very confusing place to be, and you wanted to watch your step.

Still, assuming you weren't lactose intolerant, you could survive quite nicely in the maze with enough effort.

The rats, Snitch and Scamper, used their dimwitted methods to search each and every new passageway. Snitch would try to find out if there were any rumors being passed around about where cheese might be found – frequently priming the rumor mill with lurid gossip about what the teeny people did with their teeniest parts. Snitch then passed any information along to Scamper, who would charge enthusiastically forward, crashing into the walls headfirst. As a system, it wasn't exactly elegant...but it worked often enough for the rats to survive quite nicely.

But the teeny people, Hi and Ho, preferred to use their brains to find their special Cheese. They employed complicated strategies, logical deduction, considered paradigm shifts, and listened to Tony Robbins motivational tapes, all in hopes of locating Cheese.

This system worked, but not infallibly. Sometimes the teeny peoples' emotions and ingrained habits would get in the way, and actually make the search for Cheese harder than it needed to be.

For both rats and teeny people, life in the maze was a constant challenge.

But on one very special day, Snitch, Scamper, Hi, and Ho made a wonderful discovery! Though the rats were using their instincts, and the teeny people were using their brains, all four simultaneously turned a corner and found themselves looking at CheesyWorld!

CheesyWorld was a magnificent theme park built entirely of cheese. And not just the usual cheddar, swiss, gorgonzola and roquefort. No, CheesyWorld also had plenty of capital "C" Cheese for the teeny people, which looked and tasted *exactly* like the other cheeses, but was fortified with 100% of the FDA's recommended daily dose of symbolism.

Of course, life changed for the four inhabitants of the maze. Each new day Snitch and Scamper would wake up, then make a beeline from their homes to CheesyWorld, pausing only to let Scamper get his wits back after crashing headfirst into too many walls.

Initially, Hi and Ho would also wake early and hurry into the maze, just as they had always done previously, then rapidly make their way directly to CheesyWorld. But after a few days, their teeny brains allowed them to realize that the Cheese would be there *whenever* they arrived, and there was no particular reason to hurry.

And so they started to sleep late in the mornings, linger over the sports pages, skip shaving, watch a little *Oprah*, then eventually saunter into CheesyWorld about noon – still wearing their bathrobes and slippers.

Snitch noticed this trend and thought that if he reported it there might be a bit more cheese heading his way in the future...

In the meanwhile, a most remarkable thing had happened. Because the four creatures were getting their fill of cheese every day, it was doing a very thorough job of blocking their bowels. Far from being a nuisance, this meant that they weren't constantly stepping in their own droppings anymore. Ho was so impressed by this discovery that he decided to write it on a wall, so that others might someday learn from his wisdom. He drew a big piece of cheese, and in it he wrote:

Having Cheese
Cuts Down on
All the Crap

Snitch and Scamper, having only very small brains, assumed all along that they were simply very lucky rats, having stumbled on such treasure. But Hi and Ho used their much larger brains to convince themselves that this Cheese was exactly what they deserved.

"We busted our humps for years in this maze—it's about time it paid off!" said Hi.

"I'll say," agreed Ho. "Between you and me, the Cheesegiver probably would've lost this entire maze in a hostile takeover if we hadn't been keeping things in tip-top shape!"

Meanwhile, Snitch was watching the increasingly lazy teeny people and taking notes. Notes which he would slip to Scamper on a regular basis, and which would then disappear down the hall, with only the occasional CRASH! and "Duh-h-h! *Ouch!*" to hint at Scamper's mysterious errand.

Life continued in this fashion for quite awhile, and Hi and Ho were so completely smug about their success that they were taken completely by surprise when things changed.

It was on an ordinary morning, if you consider half-past noon to be morning, and Hi and Ho were wandering sleepily down the hall in their bathrobes. As they approached the last turn to CheesyWorld, they could tell that there was something *different* in the air...

"Hey, no rat farts!" Hi noticed.

"Maybe those stupid rodents have finally wised up and decided to come in late," suggested Ho. But he couldn't have been more wrong.

Turning the corner, Hi and Ho were thunderstruck to see that CheesyWorld was a deserted ruin with no remaining Cheese and no sign of Snitch or Scamper.

Hi quickly summed up their feelings in a single word: *"AIYEEEEE!!!"*

He felt the world spinning out of control as he grew lightheaded with terror. He gasped noisily for breath.

"You're hyperventilating!" shouted Ho. "Calm down!"

"AIYEEEEEE!!!!" repeated Hi, followed by more wheezing gasps.

"Your lips are turning blue!" Ho yelled. "You're going to faint if you don't cut it out! Sit down and stick your head between your legs!"

"Will...that...make...me...feel...better?" Hi asked.

"Probably not," Ho admitted. "Try sticking your head between MY legs! *AIYEEEE!!!!"*

"AIYEEEE!!!"

The panicky screams echoed off the walls and were only barely heard by Snitch and Scamper, who had already come and gone at CheesyWorld and were now hurrying through the maze in search of new cheese. Snitch's notes had paid off, and he was sure that there would be a rich reward waiting for him somewhere. All he and Scamper had to do was find it.

Again, this might take a lot of trial and error, but being rats they had nothing but time on their feral pink hands.

Back in the wreckage of CheesyWorld, Hi and Ho had caught their breaths and were finally engaging their human brains to try to assess the situation.

Realizing that it didn't help matters to panic, Ho wrote another message on the wall. It said:

When Someone
Cuts the Cheese,
Take a Deep Breath

"So," asked Hi. "Who cut the Cheese?"

"It must've been the Cheesegiver," answered Ho. "But why?"

Hi thought about the strange situation, then his expression brightened.

"Maybe it's just a mistake—a temporary supply shortage. Sure! I'll bet the Cheese is just a little late getting here today!"

"I dunno," said Ho. "It looks like Snitch and Scamper have already given up on this place."

"They're rats!" Hi explained. "Stupid, disgusting, filthy, vermin-brained carriers of plague! Of *course* they've already moved on—they're too stupid to realize that *where Cheese was, Cheese will be again!*"

Ho wasn't sure if this was true or not, but he certainly *wanted* to believe Hi. After all, it had been a long time since he'd had to explore the maze and he wasn't sure he could do it again.

"I guess it couldn't hurt for us to wait here for awhile," he agreed.

"Sure! The Cheese will show up in no time!" Hi laughed. "Now let's just sit down and sing some songs until it gets here!"

Hours later, as night fell on the maze, the two were still singing.

"12,756 bottles of beer on the wall...12, 756 bottles of beer..."

But their voices were nearly drowned out by their growling stomachs.

Eventually, Ho said what needed to be said:

"I don't think there's any Cheese coming today."

And Hi said what *he* needed to say:

"AIYEEEEE!!!!!!!"

"Calm down!" insisted Ho, helpfully slapping Hi repeatedly. "Gather your teeny wits about you!"

"Right...right," gasped Hi. "I overreacted—sorry." Suddenly, a faint glimmer of hope appeared in Hi's eye. "I've got it! I'll bet that Cheese only gets delivered in the *mornings*. It just got missed today, but it will be here waiting for us first thing tomorrow!"

"Do you really think so?" Ho asked doubtfully.

"Absolutely!" Hi lied through his teeth. "Now let's go home."

Dragging their heels, the two shuffled back down the hallways to their homes. Eventually each of them fell fitfully asleep, dreaming of all sorts of Cheese in all sorts of submissive postures.

The next morning, they woke up earlier than they had in ages—and just for good luck, they shaved, dressed nicely, and bolted out their doors early.

They were practically running when they reached the corridor which led to CheesyWorld. Excited, they raced around the final corner and found...

"Nothing! There's no Cheese!" moaned Ho.

Remarkably, Hi did not scream "Aiyeee!"

Or maybe he did—it was pretty hard to tell since he was clutching an oxygen mask to his face. Hi's eyeballs rolled up in their sockets, leaving nothing but white showing from between the twitching eyelids. His fingernails were turning blue.

"You know, maybe this is our fault," said Ho.

"What are you talking about?" gasped Hi.

"Well, maybe we pissed off the Cheesegiver. After all, we hadn't really been performing our duties with much energy lately." Ho let this idea sink in, then continued. "Maybe the Cheesegiver thought we were just taking him for granted."

"Well, we're not anymore," Hi chuckled ruefully.

Ho felt that they'd stumbled upon another important piece of wisdom, and so he wrote his latest insight on the wall:

"Say, where do you keep finding those charcoal sticks you're using for these drawings?" Hi wondered.

"I found a whole pile of them over there where Snitch and Scamper used to sit," Ho answered. "Though it's the *softest* charcoal I've ever seen."

Hi decided to let the matter drop.

"Speaking of Snitch and Scamper," said Ho, "I wonder where they are?"

"Probably out in the maze someplace, starving to death," answered Hi.

"You know," said Ho, "They were pretty good at finding Cheese. Maybe we should consider trying their strategy."

"What—running into walls at high speed? Sure, go ahead—you first."

"No, I just meant that maybe we should get back out into the maze, too. It doesn't seem like waiting around here is doing us any good."

"You're starting to think like a rat," Hi laughed unpleasantly. "But you need to think like a teeny person. If we just stay here and do the things we've always done, sooner or later the Cheese will come back."

And so saying, Hi turned his back on Ho, and started pretending to be busy.

He penciled meetings into his Dayrunner, wrote strongly worded memos which still managed to say nothing, and loosened his tie to look harried.

"Look at me, Cheesegiver!" Hi called to no one in particular. "I sure am doing a lot of productive work here in the ol' maze today!"

Even though this sort of chicanery had always worked in the past, Ho sensed that it wouldn't anymore. Old habits were going to have to give way to new actions.

And so he picked up another stick of soft charcoal ("Gee, this stuff sort of *smells* funny, too," he thought to himself) and wrote another bit of wisdom on the wall:

Old Habits Only
Work for Old Nuns

Even knowing this, Ho was reluctant to leave his old habits behind. He was even more reluctant to leave CheesyWorld, especially because Hi seemed determined to stay.

"Maybe we're just not looking at this in the right way," Hi suggested.

"We're starving to death in a place that has no Cheese," Ho pointed out.

"Okay, that's *one* interpretation." Hi conceded. "But what if this is really just a shakeout strategy by the Cheesegiver to see who's really loyal to CheesyWorld? To see who'll stay through the hard times? Not those rats, that's for sure!"

Ho wondered if Hi's sudden attack of "loyalty" was really just a cover-up for fears and insecurities. The fact that Hi was rolling steel ball-bearings in one hand and had developed a pronounced facial tic could also, just possibly, be taken as subtle clues.

"You're over-thinking all of this," Ho blurted out. "We *both* are. I think we just need to get out and start looking for Cheese again!"

"And end up like the rats?" Hi laughed, a little too shrilly. "I can just imagine what a desperate situation *they* must be in by now!"

But actually, Hi couldn't imagine it at all. Because after a good deal of running down various blind alleys and slamming into various immovable walls, Snitch and Scamper had already reached the veritable Cheese Nirvana.

They were sitting pretty in CheesyUniverse, which was bigger, more spectacular, and had more cheese than 100 CheesyWorlds put together. There were majestic cheese towers, cheese parades, cheese marching bands, and more. At that very moment, Snitch and Scamper were enjoying more cheeses in more ways than they'd ever dreamed—and being rats, they'd never dreamed of anything else.

"Yeah, I'll bet the poor dumb bastards are *starving* by now," Hi laughed as he pulled his belt several notches tighter.

Ho had his doubts, but he remained with Hi, hoping for the best. But day turned into night, and night into day. More days passed – and still no Cheese. Finally, Ho's hunger convinced him that it was time for action.

"All of this thought and rationalization is getting us nowhere!" he shouted at Hi. "I'm going out into that maze, and I'm finding Cheese! Are you coming with me?!"

But oddly, Hi didn't answer. In fact, he seemed completely unaware of Ho's presence at all. Hi simply walked around CheesyWorld in the same old patterns, like an animal caged too long.

He kept looking in all of the places where Cheese had been and, finding none, moved on to the next spot. In Ho's mind, he was following a beautiful and seductive woman who danced just out of reach. An alluring woman with a golden radiance which was the only clue that she was formed entirely of Velveeta.

"He's totally lost it," Ho realized, waggling his fingers in front of Hi's unseeing eyes. Ho realized that he would share Hi's fate unless he finally got moving.

And hoping against hope that Hi would eventually break free of his illusions, Ho left him a message on the wall:

And so, Ho walked out into the maze and left CheesyWorld behind. He was a bit surprised to discover unexpected emotions welling up inside. Was he feeling fear, or excitement? Anxiety, or just maybe *the thrill of a bold new adventure?*

"Nope, it's fear," realized Ho as he dropped to his knees, wracked with dry heaves.

Much later, he staggered to his feet and wandered down a long corridor, which led to more corridors, which led to multiple passageways, which led to...where? The number of choices to be made stole Ho's breath away...though considering the current state of his breath, this was something of a blessing.

As Ho plodded along, he wished he had started his journey sooner. He realized he might have been better prepared to look for new Cheese if he'd only paid more attention to what had been going on at CheesyWorld. Now that he thought of it, there had been changes going on *before* the Cheese ran out.

Day by day, the Cheese wasn't stacked *quite* as high as it had been previously. And some of the Cheese wasn't as fresh as it should've been. Some of it, in fact, was so sickeningly rancid that he hadn't been sure if the Cheese was spoiled or simply French.

Yes, the signs had all been there, but Hi and Ho had used their advanced brains to rationalize the changes instead of learning from them the way Snitch and Scamper had.

Clues had been missed.

Warning signs were ignored.

Just in case anyone would follow his path in the maze, Ho wrote his latest insight on the wall:

Don't Get So Distracted
By Hope That You
Ignore The Real
Change.

Over the next several days, Ho's trip through the maze took him down many blind alleys, but also occasionally led him to small bits of Cheese. These not only nourished him, but they also encouraged him to keep searching.

"You know," he thought to himself, "This really isn't so bad. A guy could really get to enjoy..."

But his thought was abruptly cut off when Ho heard the sound of squealing tires and maniacal laughter. He turned just in time to see a scruffy looking rat speeding toward him in a tiny sports car!

A collision seemed unavoidable – but Ho threw himself against a wall and the car roared by with inches to spare.

"Gangway!" shouted the rat. "I'm on the fast track to find cheese!"

As the car disappeared into the distance, Ho angrily shook his fist in the air.

"He could've killed me!" Ho realized. "All he cared about was the Cheese, and he never even sounded his horn!"

Hoping to prevent a similar incident in the future, Ho turned to the wall and wrote a warning to other speeding rats:

As Ho started trudging down the long hallway again, he found himself getting angrier and angrier at the offending rat. And not just the insane driving.

No, what really bugged him was that the rat's car gave him an unfair advantage in getting to new Cheese faster than Ho ever could. Why, by the time Ho reached the next "CheesyWorld," that bucktoothed bastard could've been eating the Cheese for days! There might not even be any Cheese left! And if that was the case, why should Ho even continue walking?

But Ho realized he *wasn't* walking. He had stopped dead in his tracks, consumed with his envy and anger– and he hadn't even been aware of it.

"Whoa!" he thought, feeling the first stirrings of another aphorism coming on. "If you spend all your energy worrying about *others* getting ahead, then you'll have no energy left to get ahead yourself!"

He considered writing this on the wall, but decided that it wouldn't fit inside a piece of clip-art.

Instead, he took a deep breath and said: "I'll just put one foot in front of the other and keep moving forward. Maybe not as fast as that rat was going, but eventually we'll both end up at the same goal. And then...*I'll kill him.*"

This thought was so pleasing to Ho that he found himself filled with fresh motivation and energy. And savoring his homicidal fantasies, Ho struck off through the maze at a brisk clip, pausing only to write:

What Would You Do
If You Thought You
Could Get Away
With It?

Hurrying through the passageways and corridors, Ho found that he had a spring in his step. He paused briefly to take off his shoe, shake out the spring, then continued on his way with a renewed sense of optimism and much less of a limp.

Over the next few days, the fantasies of strangling the annoying rat passed, only to be replaced by fresh fantasies of shooting him. This, in turn, passed to fantasies involving knives, then chainsaws, then corrosive liquids, and eventually thermo-nuclear weapons.

But eventually even these pleasant images of mayhem were exhausted, and Ho's thoughts turned again to Cheese.

He visualized himself dining on fine Cheese. Scaling tall mountains of Cheese. Relaxing in a comfy Cheese recliner while watching his big screen high-definition Cheese TV.

He created Cheese fantasies in great detail...and eventually discovered something quite unusual.

Bit by bit, detail by detail, *these fantasies were starting to feel like reality to him.* And if he could believe in that reality with all his heart, he felt sure that those fantasies would eventually come true.

Then he thought about how far these fantasies had taken him– offering him a pleasant distraction from the rigors of his journey. Sensing that this was important, he began writing on the wall:

When Your Dreams
Become Reality,
You're Pretty Far
Gone.

"Hmmm," Ho said as he read his latest platitude. "Somehow the wording on that didn't come out quite as well as I'd hoped. Aw, screw it."

And still treading the fine line between optimism and starvation-induced psychosis, he pressed on.

Having plenty of time to think about things, he found himself wondering again why the Cheesegiver had cut the Cheese. Initially he'd been hurt and resentful. But now that he was back into the rhythm of being in the maze again, he wondered if maybe the Cheesegiver had actually done him a favor. After all, Ho was getting plenty of good exercise now. He'd shed unwanted pounds, and the acne which resulted from his cheese-clogged pores had long since cleared up. Cheddar breath? A thing of the past.

Plus, in looking for new Cheese, Ho felt that all of his senses had been sharpened and his emotions reawakened. Sometimes he felt a thrill at discovering a small morsel of Cheese, and other times he felt disappointment at finding none. But in both cases, he was feeling *something* – which was better than feeling nothing at all, which had been the case when he had all the Cheese he wanted.

"No doubt about it," Ho admitted to himself, "This change has been good for me. I was afraid of change, but I shouldn't have been."

Ho was so anxious to continue his journey, it was hard for him to stop long enough to write:

Babies Aren't the Only Ones Who Need A Change When Things Stink

"My God!" said Ho, leafing through a convenient thesaurus, "I'm having an *epiphany!*"

And indeed he was. Ho realized that it was his fear of change which had been holding him back and slowing him down since the very beginning of his long search. And now that he could accept change as something natural and good, nothing could hold him back!

Freed of his psychological chains, Ho actually sprinted through the maze, a marathon runner with the finish line in sight.

Even so, Ho was very surprised by what awaited him as he turned the very next corner of the maze...

It was CheesyUniverse!

Ho stood in the doorway, stunned by the sight of so much Cheese. Was the heavenly singing of a choir of angels only his imagination? It didn't matter—nothing did. Because CheesyUniverse was real, and it was spread before him like some unimaginable buffet.

"Snitch! Scamper!" Ho called out as he recognized his old rat companions. The two, nearly comatose from overeating, still managed to greet him.

"Br-r-r-rap!" burped Snitch.

"Pf-f-urttt!" farted Scamper.

As he reached to hold his nose, Ho couldn't help brushing away a little tear of recognition. But there would be time enough later to catch up with the others. For now, Ho was ready to enjoy the rewards of his hard work. The Cheese was his at last.

Or so he thought.

Because suddenly, a veritable stampede of rats erupted behind him. The squealing rodents knocked him to the ground and ran over him as they rushed to the Cheese. Claws raked his skin and shredded his clothes.

After what seemed an eternity, Ho felt the last rat leap off his back. Dazed, he struggled to his feet and wiped bright red blood from his mouth. But the sight of that blood was nothing compared to the sight of CheesyUniverse.

Every piece of Cheese was being gnawed by rats. They ate with manic intensity, gluttons at the ultimate feast.

"How can this be?" Ho wondered. "Where did they come from? I didn't see them on my way here!"

"Maybe," laughed Snitch, "They came a *different* way."

"What are you talking about?" Ho demanded.

"Well, how did *you* get here?" Snitch asked.

"By hard work, setting goals, accepting change, and believing in my dreams," answered Ho.

Scamper rolled onto his back, convulsed with laughter.

"Yeah," snickered Snitch, "These guys *definitely* came a different way!"

"But...what other way could there possibly be to get to the Cheese?" Ho stammered.

"As many different ways as there are different rats," sneered Snitch. "Ask around—maybe you'll learn something."

And with that, Snitch and Scamper returned to the feeding frenzy.

Ho staggered towards the horde of rats, not at all sure he wanted to hear what they had to say. Still, if he had learned nothing else, he had learned to embrace change and to be open to new ways of doing things. Perhaps the rats would have something valuable to teach him after all.

"Excuse me," Ho said to a sleek female rat. "What special skills did you use to find the Cheese?"

The rat turned her head to look at him, smiling lasciviously.

"Skills? You mean, like, work? That's so totally, like, a drag. I got what I wanted by wearing thong panties and showing the Cheesegiver my cute little tail."

"I'll be damned," Ho muttered to himself. He then wrote this newfound wisdom on a wall:

Hard Work Can't Compete With a Little Tail

Next, Ho caught the attention of a scraggly-looking gray rat.

"Would you tell me how you found the Cheese?" Ho asked.

"Wad makes you tink I cad fide cheese?" the rat replied. His skinny nose was so pinched that his speech was hard to understand. "I cad hardly smell *anyding* wid my dose."

"Well, if you can't smell Cheese," said Ho, "how *did* you get here?"

"I can'd smell cheese, but I cad smell dings dat really *stink,*" said the rat. "So I just kept my dose udder the tail of anudder rat who *could* smell cheese, ad followed hib here!"

As the rat turned away for another mouthful of limburger, Ho reflected on this latest strategy for success. Recognizing it as being important, he drew another picture on the wall:

To Succeed, Keep Your Nose Up Someone's Ass

Ho considered the things he was learning as he walked through the rapidly dwindling ruins of CheesyUniverse. Squealing, quarreling rats clung to every cheesy surface—snapping their teeth at any of their companions who came too close. It was the sort of nightmarish scene Hieronymus Bosch might have painted after tangling with a bad fondue.

"Pardon me," Ho inquired of a singularly stupid looking rat with black and white patches of fur. "May I ask you a question?"

"I don't think answering questions is part of my job description," sneered the rat. It then tapped the shoulder of a much larger rat with an identical black and white pattern. "Daddy," he whined, "Is answering questions part of my job description?"

"Certainly not!" growled the larger rat, glaring at Ho. "Who the hell are you to ask questions of my son?! I'm the *boss* of this pile of cheese, and he answers to me and me only! Now leave us alone!"

The large rat snapped his fangs at Ho, sending the teeny person running. He looked back from a safe distance to see the younger rat smirking around a mouthful of cheese.

Ho turned to a nearby wall and wrote:

You Don't Have to
Answer Questions
If You're The
Boss's Son

Ho's head was spinning from this flood of new information. It wasn't hard work that allowed these rats to succeed where he had failed, and it wasn't their willingness to accept change.

"It just takes a little tail!" Ho laughed hysterically, "Keeping your nose up someone's ass, or being the boss's son!"

Dizzy from hunger and exhaustion, Ho dropped to his knees. It dawned on him that here, in the midst of the greatest collection of Cheese anyone had ever imagined, he would soon starve to death – his complex human brain utterly defeated by the instinctive behavior of rodents.

To win the rat race, he realized, *you have to be a rat.*

Painfully, Ho crawled to a nearby wall, hoping to write his final insight. But his strength failed him. Slumped against the wall, he could feel his consciousness slipping away. His eyes fluttered briefly before closing. The echoing sound of the rats' squeaky laughter would be the last thing he would ever hear.

Or would it...?

"MEOW!!!"

What was *that?*

"MEOW!!!"

There it was again– and now, Ho also heard the screams of terrified rats! With great effort he opened his eyes, only to discover a scene of complete chaos and horror.

A gigantic cat, many times the size of the rats (or a teeny person!) had somehow found its way into CheesyUniverse, and it was ripping the rodents to shreds!

"This could be entertaining," Ho thought as he watched Snitch's head roll past.

The shrieking rats dived off of the cheese towers and ran—but to no avail. The cat's fangs and claws made short work of them.

"MEOW!!!" came the cry again, and a thousand ratty tails whipped aside for terror-induced projectile turds.

Blood and bits of rat flew in all directions...as did the few shrieking survivors, desperate to find their way back into the maze. Within moments, the last of the rats disappeared from view.

"Terrific!" said Ho.

"MEOW!!!" said the giant cat, glaring down at Ho with glowing eyes.

Having no tail to move, Ho's terror-induced projectile turd got only as far as his Dockers.

As the cat raised a huge, well-spiked paw, Ho closed his eyes and waited for the fatal blow.

"Hold it!" shouted a familiar voice, "He's with me!"

Huh? Had the cat actually spoken?

Ho opened his eyes and looked up at the cat, only to see Hi sitting astride the beast's neck!

"Nice place you've got here!" Hi laughed as he dropped to the ground. "Plenty of Cheese under all the turds and blood!"

"I...I thought you were dead!" Ho stammered. "Didn't you starve to death?"

"No, no," explained Hi, "I was right all along! The Cheesegiver appreciated my unthinking loyalty and started sending Cheese again right after you left. In fact, I got a nice raise out of it!"

"Then what are you doing *here?"* Ho asked.

"Looking for you, old buddy. Life in the maze is tough, and I figured that the rats might be giving you a hard time. That's why I hired a little muscle here."

Hi stood on his tiptoes to scratch the chin of the gigantic cat and was rewarded with a purr that rumbled like distant thunder.

"Hired?" Ho repeated. "Who did you hire him *from?* And with *what?"*

"I hired him from the Cheesegiver," Hi explained. "Turns out he's a lot like us, only he's really big and works in a University testing lab. And because he's chronically underpaid, I just gave him some of this!"

Hi pulled a large canvas bag off the cat's back and opened it to reveal piles of green paper inside.

"I found a bunch of this back in CheesyWorld. It's called 'money' and Big People are just *crazy* about it," said Hi. "C'mon now, let's get you to your feet and go have some Cheese."

Propped up by his old friend, his new hopes, and a better understanding of the larger world around him, Ho got to his feet. But before heading to the long-awaited Cheese, he paused to write one final truth on the wall.

And it was the greatest truth of them all:

The End....

*....or is it the beginning of more padding
to make this seem like a real book?*

Another Round, Bartender
Later That Night

As Biff finished speaking, he could tell by his friends' smiling faces that they'd enjoyed the story and several more rounds of drinks.

"It gives you a lot to think about, doesn't it?" he asked.

"I'll say," said Norman. "Wha's the deal with these teeny people? I mean is that some sorta genetic experiment gone wrong, or a cloning thing, or *what?* Is there some secret laboratory doin' this shtuff?"

"Don't forget the talking rats," added Michelle.

"How could I?" shivered Norman. "If one of *those* babies ever turns up inside a BaggaBurger bun, it's my ash for sure. *(*hiccup*)*"

"You're taking this too literally," Biff said, his smile a bit forced. "The story didn't really happen. It's an *allegory.*"

Norman's brow furrowed as he tossed back a shot of tequila. "Wha's an allegory?"

"It's like a crocodile," Naomi joked, "Only with a pointed nose."

"Oh-h-h-h," Norman nodded his head. "I get it! An allegory is a crock...but with a *point!*"

"I couldn't have put it better myself," agreed Biff. "And the way to learn from the story is to think about which of the four characters is the most like you."

"I'm definitely not a Snitch," said Michelle. "Snitch always had ways of finding out the inside information and being ready for a change. At my job, we had no idea that changes in technology were making our product obsolete...and when our factory closed, we were all taken completely by surprise!"

"What were you making?" Norman wondered.

"Slide rules, mostly," Michelle sighed. "The abacus market in China pretty much went to hell, too. But back then, who could possibly have known that computers would really catch on?"

"Back when?" Naomi asked.

"Christmas of '99," Michelle answered. "Man, we sure didn't see THAT market trend coming."

She shook her head to clear it, then reached for the bowl of snacks by Biff's elbow. "Mind sharing your nuts?" she asked with a wry smile.

"Anytime," laughed Biff. "Just don't let my wife cashew!"

By a prearranged agreement, the penalty for a particularly bad pun was the price of another round of drinks.

"How about you, Norman?" asked Michelle. "Which character were you?"

"I sure wasn't Scamper," he muttered, wobbling a bit. "That bashtard took off like a rocket—ZHOOM!—and away he went. Din'nt matter if he ran inta this—*wham!*—or inta that—*bam!* Nah, that little sonofabitch jus' kept on runnin' and runnin' and runnin' after that cheese. He knew he's gonna get somewhere someday, not like me. Not like ol' Normal Normie. Not goin' anywhere."

Norman fished a piece of ice out of his glass and rubbed it across his forehead, trying to erase some inner pain.

"I have thish strange dream, again and again," he explained. "I'm workin' the lunch shift, and everything's goin' to hell, and then thish creepy voice comes through the shpeaker for the drive-thru window. I don't know what it says, but suddenly all these zit-faced uniformed kids are grabbing me—my own employees—and they shove my head into the deep fryer! Sizzlin' like a bastard—smoke fillin' the air! I'm kickin' and screamin', but the oil just boils my tongue, y'know? Finally they pull me out, and my whole damn head is a crispy critter. And they stick my head in a bag and take it to the drive-thru window—an' you know who'sh inna damn car?! *The Grim Frickin' Reaper!* An' he paysh the bill, and then you know what he *says?* Do ya?! He says KEEP THE CHANGE!!!!"

The group was momentarily still, considering Norman's words and discreetly checking out the nearest exits. Then Naomi tactfully broke the silence.

"What in the *hell* are you talking about, Norman?"

"Change! Aren't we talkin' 'bout how scary change is?"

"*Sure* we are, Norman," Bill said reassuringly—then whispered to the waitress, "Just ginger ale for this guy, okay babe?"

"Now where were we?" prompted Naomi. "Michelle said she wasn't like Snitch, because she wasn't aware of change coming. And Norman said he wasn't like Scamper, because fear of change kept him from scampering to a better job."

"Which character would you like to be?" purred Biff as he fed Naomi a maraschino cherry.

"Well," answered Naomi, "I guess I'd like to be more of a Ho."

"As if *that* were possible," muttered Michelle.

"I beg your pardon?!" snapped Naomi.

"I said, *that* sounds very responsible," Michelle quickly adlibbed. "You know, making a real effort to change and all."

"Oh. Well...thank you. Besides, I don't think that any of us wants to be Hi."

"Shpeak for yourself," groused Norman, "Wha's in these effin' drinks anyway—ginger ale?!"

Chuckling, Biff explained, "I think she meant the teeny man in the story named Hi. The one who failed to embrace change and move ahead with his life. You know, when I first happened upon the story of *Who Cut The Cheese,* I bought copies for everyone in my company to read—and then we all got together to discuss which of the four characters we were most like. As you would expect, most of the *Snitchs* and *Scampers* had jobs in management, either predicting change and then getting the hell out of the way, or running blindly ahead without the *least* idea of where they were going. And of course, all of them were up to their asses in Cheese!"

This got a good laugh of recognition from the table.

"But we found out that there were a lot of *Ho* types, too—people who had been doing things the same way for so long that they'd forgotten what change was like. But after hearing the story of *Who Cut The Cheese,* they were so eager to rediscover the reinvigorating qualities of change that they all quit on the spot—and a lot of them mooned management, too!"

"So the only ones left to do any real work were the *Hi* types, right?" asked Michelle.

"Not exactly. You see, the management was so impressed by the story of *Who Cut The Cheese* that they considered the *Hi* types to be losers—so they fired the lot of them. Security dragged them kicking and screaming into the parking lot and then fired a few shots over their heads to run 'em off."

"Waitaminnit, waitaminnit," said Norman, sniffing his glass suspiciously. "If your company got rid of everybody but the idiots in *management,* how the hell could they shtay in business?"

"They couldn't!" admitted Biff. "The company folded in less than three weeks, the stockholders filed a lawsuit, and everyone in management went to jail! I was lucky to get off with a fine and some community service as a flosser at the homeless dental clinic."

"Well, you TOLD us that this Cheese story had changed your life," sighed Michelle. "I just wish you'd been a little more *specific* three hours ago."

"Yeah," agreed Naomi, slamming her legs together and pushing Biff's hand away. "I thought you said you were making big money?"

"Like never before!" laughed Biff. "I'm selling copies of *Who Cut the Cheese* out of the back of my car—and I'm making thousands of dollars!"

"Really? Tell me more," Naomi purred as she inadvertently pressed her room key into Biff's hand.

"*Who Cut the Cheese* is selling like hotcakes—anyone who hears it wants a copy for himself, and probably a few dozen copies to give as gifts. Corporate sales are even better—you can make hundreds of sales with a single call!"

"Wow!" exclaimed Michelle. "And just imagine the sales I could make if I also include a free slide rule or abacus!"

"I'm in, too!" sloshed Norman. "To hell with the hamburgersh and greash and teenagersh and the Grim Reaper and..." Norman's head thudded heavily to the table as he slipped into an alcoholic coma.

"You heard him say he was in, right?" Biff queried the ladies. "That's a verbal contract that'll stand up in any court."

On the far side of the room, the bartender checked his watch then lifted a shotgun from behind the bar to indicate that closing time had come.

"I'm certainly glad you told us the story of *Who Cut the Cheese,*" enthused Michelle. "My whole life will be immeasurably better now."

"There's no question that *Who Cut the Cheese* is the most profound and inspiring story ever written," agreed Naomi as she rummaged through her purse for her diaphragm.

"I'm delighted that you found the story so helpful," said Biff as he paid the substantial bar tab from Norman's wallet. "And I hope that *millions* of other Americans will also enjoy better lives after purchasing *Who Cut the Cheese* at better bookstores everywhere!"

The End

Spread The Cheese!

Why not buy more copies of this book right now, and sell them at a significant markup to your co-workers, unemployed friends, and complete strangers?

Who Cut The Cheese?

Order Form:

Quantity to purchase_____

Oh come on, You want more than *that*_____

That's More Like It_____

Name_____

Address_____

City_____ State_____ Zip _____

Method of Payment:

      [ ] Check

      [ ] Cheese

      [ ] Charge Card   Number_____

      Expiration Date_____

Author, Author!

Stilton Jarlsberg, M.D. has made vast professional strides, which is an impressive accomplishment considering that he is only 6 inches tall. By virtue of this fact, he was awarded a scholarship to medical school so that he might actually participate in experiments alongside lab rats as a human "control." His experience with mazes and cheesy rewards speaks volumes about the expertise he brings to the book you currently hold in your hands.

His previous book, *The One Minute Mangler*, was originally the story of a psychotic, brutally sadistic serial killer and sold fewer than a dozen copies. However, when he realized that many of the psycho killer's torture techniques could be successfully applied to the business world, the book was re-edited and released as a non-fiction management manual, at which time it became a huge international bestseller.

Following this unexpected success, Stilton Jarlsberg has published an entire series of *"One Minute"* books, and hopes to eventually see them turned into a series of big budget feature films for people with exceedingly short attention spans.

Made in the USA
San Bernardino, CA
17 December 2017